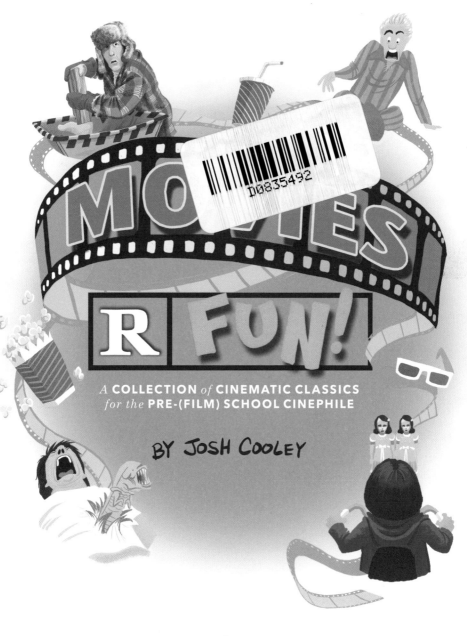

MOVIES R FUN!

A COLLECTION *of* CINEMATIC CLASSICS
for the PRE-(FILM) SCHOOL CINEPHILE

BY JOSH COOLEY

CHRONICLE BOOKS
SAN FRANCISCO

For my kids . . . who will never be allowed to read this book.

Library of Congress Cataloging-in-Publication Data
Cooley, Josh.
  Movies r fun! : a collection of Cinematic classics for the Pre-(film) school Cinephile/ Josh Cooley.
     pages cm
  ISBN 978-1-4521-2233-5
  1. Motion pictures—Juvenile humor. I. Title.

  PN1994.5.C66 2013
  791.43—dc23
                    2013010809

Manufactured in Canada

Illustrated by Josh Cooley
Designed by Erin Cooley and Michael Morris

10 9 8 7 6 5 4 3

Chronicle Books LLC
680 Second Street
San Francisco, California 94107
www.chroniclebooks.com

"This would sharpen you up
and make you ready for a bit of the
old ultraviolence," explained Alex.

"Say what again. Say **what** again,"
said Jules.
"I dare you, I double dare you."

"You want a toe? I can get you a toe,"
said Walter.
"Hell, I can get you a toe by 3 o'clock
this afternoon, with nail polish."

"I'm gonna make him an offer he can't refuse,"
explained Don Corleone.

"I want you to hit me," said Tyler Durden,
"as hard as you can."

"I want to buy your women,"
explained Jake.
"Sell them to me. Sell me your children!"

"You are a very nosey fella, kitty kat, huh?"
asked the midget.
"You know what happens to nosey fellas?"

"Whose money do I have?"
asked the driver.

"I'm sorry, Dave," said Hal.
"I'm afraid that I cannot do that."

"Police! Freeze!" said Marge.
"WRRRRRRRRRRRRRR..."
went the woodchipper.

"Your clothes . . . give them to me, now,"
said the Terminator.

"Hi, Brad. You know how cute I always thought you were," said Linda.

"Now go home and get your #$@&*% shinebox!"
suggested Billy Batts.

"Me so horny," explained the lady.
"Me love you long time."

"Kane, what is it? What is wrong?" asked Ripley.
"AAAAHHHHHhhhhhh!" answered Kane.

"What's the most you've ever lost
on a coin toss?" asked Anton.

"Pause," went the VCR.

"Wait . . . what is happening?"
asked the audience.

"He got a real purty mouth, ain't he?"
said the mountain man.

"Wolfie is fine, honey . . . Wolfie's just fine,"
said the T-1000. "Where are you?"

"What have you done to it?"
asked Rosemary.
"What have you done to its eyes?"

"Yippee-Kay-Yay mother #@&*$%!"
said John McClane.

"Would you like me to seduce you?"
asked Mrs. Robinson.
"Is that what you are trying to tell me?"

"Eeny, meeny, miny, moe,"
said Hit-Girl.

"I want to be a cleaner, just like you,"
said Mathilda.
"Okay," replied Léon.

"The power of Christ compels you!"
commanded Father Damien.

"I can do anything I want,"
explained Frank.
"And so can you."

"Come play with us, Danny,"
said the twins.
"For ever . . . and ever . . . and ever."

"¡Ay, no me gusta!"
thought Ofelia.

"It rubs the lotion on its skin,
or else it gets the hose again,"
explained Buffalo Bill.

"Run! Go! Git to da choppah!"
screamed Ahnold.

"Spec-tac-u-lar!"
thought Lester Burnham.

"Just walk away," said The Lord Humungus.
"Give me your pump, the oil, the gasoline,
and I'll spare your lives. Just walk away."

"Four . . . three . . . two . . . one . . .
I am now authorized to use
physical force!" warned ED-209.

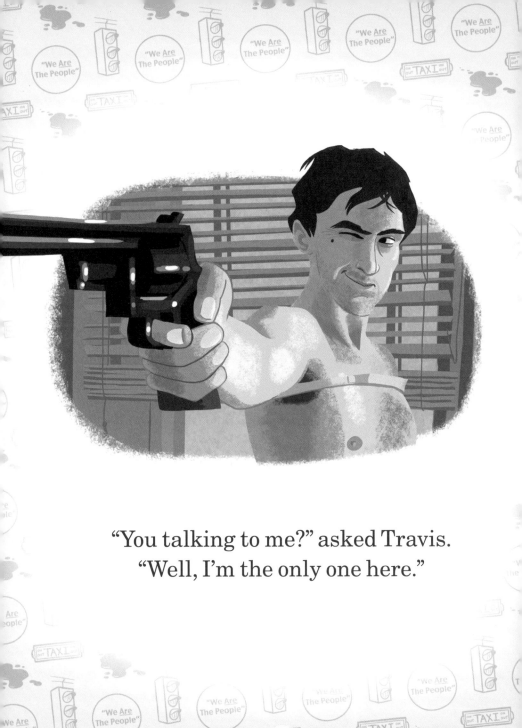

"You talking to me?" asked Travis.
"Well, I'm the only one here."

"You're gonna need a bigger boat,"
suggested Chief Brody.

"Eek, Eek, Eek, Eek, Eek!"
went the orchestra.

"You gotta be %@#&* kidding,"
said Palmer.

"What is in the box? What is in the box?"
asked Detective Mills.

"The horror . . . the horror . . ."
gasped Colonel Kurtz.